A CHILD'S DAY
IN A RUSSIAN CITY

To my father, who gave me my very first camera

Benchmark Books
Marshall Cavendish
99 White Plains Road
Tarrytown, New York 10591
Website:www.marshallcavendish.com

Library of Congress Cataloging-in-Publication Data

Ilyin, Andrey.
In a Russian city / by Andrey Ilyin.
p. cm. — (A child's day)
Includes index.
ISBN 0-7614-1222-0
1. Russia (Federation)—Social life and customs—1991—-Juvenile literature.
[1. Russia (Federation)—Social life and customs.] I. Title. II. Series.

DK510.32 .I47 2001   947.086—dc21   00-068073

Designed by Sophie Pelham

Printed in Singapore

1 3 5 7 9 8 6 4 2

AUTHOR ACKNOWLEDGMENTS
With thanks to Polina Lesnevitch and her family for making this book possible.

A CHILD'S DAY
IN A RUSSIAN CITY

Andrey Ilyin

BENCHMARK BOOKS

MARSHALL CAVENDISH
NEW YORK

AUTHOR'S NOTE

RUSSIA

St. Petersburg

Polina and her family are Peterburdgets, the name given to people who live in Saint Petersburg. Saint Petersburg has played a very important role in Russia's history, and was Russia's capital city for more than two hundred years (until Moscow took over this job in 1914).

Over the last century, Saint Petersburg has changed its name three times—from Saint Petersburg to Petrograd, to Leningrad, and then back to Saint Petersburg again—but it was originally named after Peter the Great, the Russian emperor who founded the city about three hundred years ago. Peter described his new capital as a "window on Europe" because of its unique position on the coast of the Baltic Sea, looking across to Europe.

Polina is a city girl: she lives in a high-rise apartment building and is used to lots of noise and traffic. But just like Russians everywhere, she has a very close-knit family. Both Polina's parents need to work full-time, but her grandparents live right next door, and Polina spends time with them every day.

Polina is seven years old.

She lives with her parents in a small apartment on the twelfth floor of a sixteen-story apartment building in Saint Petersburg. Polina's grandparents live in the apartment next door. Polina's mother, Natalia, works as a cashier at the local supermarket, and Polina's father, Alexey, is a refrigerator repairman.

As soon as she wakes up, Polina jumps out of bed and rushes to the shower. This is her favorite part of the morning, and even though her mother has called her for breakfast twice already, Polina is pretending she can't hear so she can continue washing!

6

For a treat Polina's mother has prepared some *bliny* and *smetana* for breakfast today instead of the usual porridge. It's just the two of them because Polina's father has already had to leave for work.

BLINY are traditional Russian pancakes, made out of buckwheat flour and yeast. They can be served with all sorts of different fillings, such as smetana (a kind of sour cream), melted butter, ham, or even caviar (fish eggs).

Polina loves reading, so she goes to the library whenever she can. This morning she is the first person in the reading room and she has chosen a brand-new book. It still has that fresh inky smell from the printers.

The librarian records the book on Polina's *formular* (library card). Readers are allowed to keep books for two weeks, but Polina likes the look of this one so much, she'll probably finish it in a couple of days.

There's still some time before classes start. Polina and her friends
do some chalk drawings on the pavement outside the library.

Polina is never late for school. By nine o'clock she and her class-mates are in the classroom with their textbooks and notebooks all ready. Before they start, the teacher takes attendance and checks everyone's homework.

The first lesson of the day is Russian. The teacher asks for volunteers to come up to the board, but only the bravest ones in the class put up their hands.

Each lesson lasts for forty-five minutes but sometimes that seems too long, so the teacher announces a break to play *slova*.

SLOVA means "words" in Russian. The idea of this game is to make up as many words as possible using the letters of one very long word, which the teacher chooses.

Next they play *ladoshki* (palms).

LADOSHKI The children split into twos and stand facing each other. When the teacher says "Go," they push each other's palms to try to make the other person lose his or her balance. It's not just a game of strength: if you are clever, you can fool your opponent by pretending that you are about to push really hard but instead suddenly pulling back so that the other person topples into you.

The first lesson after lunch is crafts. Polina's classmate is making a colorful vase out of an old glass jar, plasticine, and a mixture of kidney beans and peas.

The last lesson of the day is religious studies. The teacher shows the class slides of churches from different parts of Russia. These people are lighting candles and saying prayers for their families and friends.

The saint in this painting is believed to protect the church and all the people who pray there.

The sound of *kolokola* (bells) can be heard all over Saint Petersburg several times a day.

KOLOKOLA Russian bell ringing isn't like bell ringing in Europe, because Russian church bells play rhythms (like drumbeats) rather than tunes. Russian bells are also much lighter than European ones, which means one person can play lots of bells at the same time.

15

After school Polina and her mother catch the streetcar into the center of Saint Petersburg. Here they are passing over one of the hundreds of bridges in the city. Sometimes Saint Petersburg is called "Northern Venice" because, just like the famous city of Venice in Italy, so many rivers and waterways flow through it.

Whenever she walks by, Polina can't resist playing with this stone sphere. It is supported by a thin layer of water, so even though the stone is very heavy, Polina can rotate it easily.

In one of the squares near *Nevsky Prospekt*, a street artist gives Polina a quick lesson on portrait drawing.

NEVSKY PROSPEKT is the main street of Saint Petersburg. People spend a long time walking along it because there are so many old buildings to admire and interesting shops to visit.

Art can be hard work—
Polina decides it's time
for ice cream!

When her mother
isn't looking, Polina
buys her some flowers
as a present.

19

Back home, Polina gets together with some of her friends for a game of catch.

They play *klassy* (hopscotch) too.

20

Then Polina and her friend Katya have an idea. They run inside to tell Polina's grandfather about it, and he finds them some paper, cotton, and plywood.

When their new kite is ready, Polina, Katya, and their friend Hayal, who lives nearby, run back to the park to try it out.

Later, Polina goes to her theater group at the local arts center.

To warm up, the children play a memory game called *ovetchya golova* (sheep head). The first person to make a mistake gets called *"ovetchya golova"* by the rest of the group.

Today's rehearsal is the last one before the play will be performed in front of an audience. To wish his cast good luck, the leader of the theater group has brought some *arbuz* (watermelon).

It is late already but Polina has some homework to do before tomorrow. First she has to copy some sentences from her textbook and underline the adjectives in each one.

The second homework assignment is more difficult: Polina has to write a short story about somewhere in Russia she would like to visit. She chooses Lake Baikal, the deepest lake in the world. It is in an area of Russia called Siberia.

When Polina has finished her homework, the family gathers around the *samovar* (a kind of water heater) for tea.

SAMOVARS were first made in Russia about a hundred years ago, and they are specially designed to boil water quickly and easily. Once the tea has been made, the teapot is put on top of the samovar so that the tea inside stays hot.

Before she goes to bed, Polina's grandma reads her a bedtime story.

Spokoinoi nochi, Polina (Good night, Polina).

MORE ABOUT RUSSIA

Russia is the largest country in the world. It stretches like a giant umbrella from Europe all the way across Asia to the United States. It's so big that even if you caught a plane, it would take you ten hours to travel from one end of the country to the other. By train, the same journey would take at least a week, so you would get plenty of time to look out the window and watch the scenery rushing by. Russia has many different kinds of landscapes: dry desert in the southwest of the country, large areas of forest in the north, and a vast treeless zone near the North Pole (called the tundra), where the ground is frozen solid all year round.

RUSSIA, THE PAST

For hundreds of years Russia was ruled by powerful emperors called czars (pronounced *zars*). But in 1917 two important revolutions took place that changed Russia forever. The first, the February Revolution, was led by a group of Russians who thought the whole system of czars was unfair. They forced the czar of the time to give up his power and set up a new government instead. The second, the October Revolution, was organized by the Bolsheviks. These people didn't like the new government and so they put a different one in its place. After that Russia became a Communist country, and life for ordinary Russian people was often difficult. Under the Communist system, they had to get special permission to travel abroad, and if they went to church or even read books that the Communist rulers didn't like, they risked severe punishment.

But these harsh times didn't last forever. In 1991 the Communists lost their power. Russia is no longer separate from the rest of the world, and everyday life for the Russian people has changed once again.

RELIGION IN RUSSIA

Most Russians are Orthodox Christians, and Easter is one of the biggest holidays of the year. In almost every home, people make a special onion broth and paint the shells of hard-boiled eggs to give them a beautiful ocher (yellowy orange) color. When guests arrive, they are greeted with the exclamation, "Christ has arisen!" and given a painted egg as a present.

PEOPLE IN RUSSIA

The best thing about Russia is the people who live there. Russian people are full of energy and ideas, which is why there have been so many Russian writers, artists, and scientists throughout history. The Russian writers Leo Tolstoy and Anton Chekhov are famous all over the world. Although they wrote their books and plays a long time ago, their stories can still tell us a lot about the mystery of what it is to be human.

Russians love to read, whether it's Tolstoy, Chekhov, or the daily newspaper. On the subway in Moscow in rush hour, you can always see people sandwiched next to one another with their heads buried in a book. In fact, reading in Russia is probably almost as popular as ice-cream eating—and that's saying a lot because Russians are crazy about ice cream! There are hundreds of ice-cream stands in every town, and people enjoy it even in the depths of *zima* (winter) when the air outside in the streets is as icy cold as the ice cream itself.

LANGUAGE IN RUSSIA

If you opened up a Russian book, the first thing you would notice is that all the letters are different from the ones used to write English. That's because Russian has a completely different alphabet: English is made up of twenty-six letters and starts with *a, b, c*, whereas the Russian alphabet has thirty-two letters and starts with а, б, в. (The Russian words in this book have been written using the English alphabet so that you can read them.)

As well as the Russian alphabet being longer, most Russian words are longer than English ones, which means Russian books are longer too. The long words make it quite difficult to write pop songs in Russian, but they are perfectly suited to the slow melodies of Russian folk music. When you listen to these old songs, it is easy to imagine Russia's vast open spaces and long, cold winters.

All schoolchildren in Russia learn English because that way they will be able to talk to people from other countries when they are older. Russians also borrowed some words from English, especially ones to do with technology—such as *kompjuter* and *aeroplan*—and made them their own. You can probably guess what they mean!

SOME RUSSIAN WORDS AND PHRASES

privet (pree-*vyet*)—hello
dobroye utro (*dob*-row-yeh *uh*-tro)—
    good morning
Kak dela? (kak de-*lah*)—How are you?
Kotoriy chas? (ko-*to*-ree chas)—
    What is the time?
spasibo (spa-*see*-boh)—thank you
do svidania (do svee-*dah*-nyah)—
    good-bye

THE RUSSIAN WORDS IN THE BOOK

aeroplan–airplane

Anton Chekhov–a famous Russian playwright
who was born in 1860 and died in 1904.
One of his most well-known plays is
The Cherry Orchard.

arbuz–watermelon

bliny–traditional Russian pancakes, which can
be served with many different fillings

Bolshevik–the old name for a member of
the Russian Communist Party

czar–the title that was given to Russian emperors

formular–library card

klassy–hopscotch

kolokola–bells

kompjuter–computer

ladoshki–"palms," a classroom game

Lake Baikal–a large lake in Siberia

Leo Tolstoy–a famous Russian writer who was
born in 1828 and died in 1910. His two most
well-known books are *Anna Karenina* and
War and Peace.

Nevsky Prospekt–Nevsky Avenue, the main
street in Saint Petersburg

ovetchya golova–"sheep head," a memory game

Peterburdgets–the name given to people who
come from the city of Saint Petersburg

samovar–a special Russian water heater used
to make tea and keep it hot

Siberia–a vast region of Russia

slova–"words," a classroom game

smetana–a kind of sour cream, often served as
a filling with bliny

Spokoinoi nochi–Good night

zima–the Russian winter, which lasts from the
end of November to the end of March

FIND OUT MORE

Arnold, Helen. *Russia.* Austin, Texas: Raintree Steck-Vaughn, 1990.

Franco, Betsy. *Around the World: Russia.* Monterey, California: Evan-Moor, 1993.

Nickles, Greg and Bobbie Kalman. *Russia the Culture.* New York: Crabtree Publishing, 2000.

INDEX